Join Generations: Becoming Unashamedly Intergenerational
©2013 by Matthew Donald Deprez

Published in the United States by AtlantiCreative

ISBN: 978-1-304-66743-4

All rights reserved. No portion of this book may be reproduced, stored in a retrieval system, or transmitted in any form or by any other means – electronic, mechanical, photocopy, recording, or other – except for brief quotations in critical reviews or articles, without the prior written permission of the author or publisher.

Edited by Kelsey Jones

Author Photography by Bradley James Photography

Cover and Interior Design by Joshua Harris of AtlantiCreative.com
Cover and Design ©2013 Joshua Harris

Unless otherwise marked, Scripture quotations are taken from *The Holy Bible, New International Version.* Copyright 1973, 1978, 1984 by International Bible Society. Used by permission of Zondervan. All rights reserved.

Library of Congress Cataloging-in-Publication Data
Deprez, Matthew Donald
Join Generations: Becoming Unashamedly Intergenerational / Matthew Donald Deprez
1. Church. 2. Intergenerational. 3. Christianity. 4. Christian Living.
5. Discipleship. 6. Faith 7. Religion

Printed in the United States of America

Join Generations

BECOMING UNASHAMEDLY INTERGENERATIONAL

MATTHEW DEPREZ

Praise for Join Generations

"A must-read for any youth pastor, whether you're fresh out of seminary or a seasoned veteran. Matthew Deprez clearly articulates what becomes possible when we embrace intergenerational ministry, and what's at stake if our youth ministries continue isolating students from the rest of the Church."

- Kenny Campbell, Co-Founder of stuffyoucanuse.org & Middle School Pastor, The Chapel at CrossPoint, Buffalo, NY

"Anytime I'm asked what's the newest and greatest thing in youth ministry, I always refer to Matthew Deprez's work on becoming intergenerational. The ironic thing is, there is nothing new about this. There's no program to download, no new formula to implement, in fact, what Matthew is suggesting will sound wildly old school to some. Matthew takes seriously the priesthood of all believers and rightly assumes that God is able to speak to an 8-year-old as well as an 80-year-old—and yet, he does this in a way that doesn't diminish the role of the youth pastor as more recent literature has a tendency to do. Matthew has done a huge service to the universal church by sharing these insights and every pastor, regardless of their titles, will benefit from this read!"

- Dr. Amanda Drury, Assistant Professor of Youth Ministry, Indiana Wesleyan University

"Matthew has a big view of the Church and its function. In his book he clearly lays out what he believes about the need for the Church to function as a complete body, from the cradle to the grave. Matthew's voice is important in the world of Intergenerational Ministry, as he is passionate about bringing the body together to serve each other, and to be a light on a hill for the world to see. I have given this book to my team to read, which has opened up conversations for our church and our context."

- Josh Barton, Middle School Pastor, Mission Community Church, Gilbert, AZ

"Matthew Deprez's book is a vibrant contribution to the current discussion surrounding intergenerational ministries. Most churches of every size and worship style has unknowingly created silo-ministries; where children, youth and adults go on the faith-journey as separate islands surrounded by Gospel sea. Matt firmly yet graciously alerts us to the reality and the inherent dangers of this state of ministry affairs. His conversational writing-style is welcoming, his biblical foundation is solid, and his practical insights blended with actual success stories place the "next steps" for any pastor on the lower shelf. I would like to say that Matt is forward thinking. But in actuality, he is looking back to the true vision that Christ had for His Church; "That they be one as we are one." This book will drive any pastor to his knees as we consider the move from maintaining programs to assist Christ in forming His family."

- Dr. David Smith, Vice President for Academic Affairs, Kingswood University

"The ease and wisdom with which Matthew is able to communicate the practicalities of intergenerational ministry has significantly shaped my ministry paradigms. Join Generations has given me a familiar cultural vocabulary with the ancient biblical narrative in a way that allows me to communicate these simple, yet significant, discipleship practices to other pastors, volunteers, parents, and elders within my church."

- Evan Kolding, Student Ministries Director, Moraga Valley Presbyterian Church, Moraga, CA

"I am a firm believer in Intergenerational Ministry and I am so thankful Matthew has written a book about it. Looking back on the years of my life I now believe I was part of a church that did intergenerational ministry, but they probably didn't realize that was what they were doing. As a teenager I was given many opportunities to serve in ministries that involved the younger and older generations. I found such joy in serving Jesus, and because of this joy I wanted to continue serving him into my adult life. I have two grandchildren that are now serving in the Children's ministry at Frontline Church and

I am so thankful that they get to experience the joy of serving Jesus as I did as a teen and continue to do as a grandma."

- Deb Chapman, Retired Children's Ministry Director and Grandmother of 11.

Acknowledgements:

Megan and Isaiah - Megan, knowing I get to spend the rest of my life with you is the greatest joy I'll ever have. Thank you for showing me what selfless love really is. Isaiah, you're only 2.5 years old, but you display love to Mommy and me like nobody else I know. Thank you for being an example of how we can learn to follow Jesus from those who are younger than us

Mom and Dad - It's way easier to write a book about joining generations when I have parents like you who have modeled love and selflessness on such a consistent basis. You both make me look forward to aging so I can attempt to do the same thing to others that you've done for me.

Frontline Church - Five years ago, I came to Frontline extremely bitter and cynical toward the "Church." Over those years, you have restored hope in the church for me. You taught me what happens when the church values people over programs. Thank you for being the guinea pigs to expose these thoughts and stories to the world.

Kara Powell and Brad Griffin - Thank you for journeying with me and Frontline as we've walked into this exciting and terrifying road of becoming unashamedly intergenerational. I literally can't express how much you guys, and the Fuller Youth Institute, have changed my life. My family, and our church, are both better off because of you.

Joshua Harris - Thank you for all the hard work you've done to make all the creative elements of this book a reality. Also, thank you for exposing me to vegetarian nachos. LIFE-CHANGING!

Kelsey Jones - Thank you for editing countless manuscripts and editions of this book, especially when I gave you annoyingly tight deadlines.

To everybody else who has personally taught me what it means to be unashamedly intergenerational. May we continue to join generations together.

Join: To bring in contact, to connect or put together. Typically safe and something we all long to do.

Generations: Groups of individuals typically separated by age, sharing different values, ideas and beliefs. Often unsafe and loaded with implications.

Welcome to the paradox of *Joining Generations*.

Table of Contents

Foreword 15

Preface 19

Part One: Looking Backward 23

Part Two: Looking Upward 45

Part Three: Looking Forward 71

Additional Resources 121

About the Author 122

Foreword

Tonight my family is hosting our small group meeting at our house. We started this small group with three other families four years ago.

There is a family in our life stage—with kids in elementary school, middle school, and high school.

There is a family ten years younger—still having babies.

Then there is a married couple—who are both over seventy years old.

It's the best small group I've ever experienced.

It's not the quietest, most orderly, nor most calm. In the middle of lofty discussions about kingdom living, we are often interrupted by a hungry two year-old or a fifteen year-old who just remembered a homework assignment she's got to finish by tomorrow. We sometimes have to eat our brownie dessert quickly because it's thirty minutes past the five-year-old's bedtime and he's melting down.

So what makes this small group the best? It's our commitment to Jesus and to each other, and that those commitments extend across generations.

Sure, it's a bit messier than other small groups (and I mean that both figuratively and literally, as our dining room floor after dinner tonight will attest). But it's partly the mess that makes it so good. So normal. So real.

Matthew Deprez understands the beauty of the mess that is sometimes involved in intergenerational relationships. A mutual ministry friend introduced me to Matthew a number of years ago as our Sticky Faith research was highlighting the power of intergenerational relationships in long-term faith for young people. I was immediately struck not only by Matthew's passion for the church, but also by his wisdom, authenticity, and ability to invite other people into not only his life but also relationship with Jesus.

As our team at the Fuller Youth Institute has gotten to know Matthew, we've become even more impressed. He is not just talking about the future of the church; he is prayerfully working to make that future a reality.

I'm thrilled that Matthew has written Join Generations and has grounded it in some of the best research on relationships, some of the most relevant Scripture on discipleship, and some of his own experiences at Frontline Community Church. His insights and his stories have widened and deepened my own vision for what happens when you bring seven, seventeen, and seventy year-olds together. He has made me not only want to work more diligently toward intergenerational relationships, but also pray more fervently that God would unite His church.

Join Generations is an invitation to you to join in God's work in the church that extends across the generations. As we will experience in my intergenerational small group in a few hours, it's not just the young people who are being changed. All of us are being changed.

- **Dr. Kara Powell,**
Executive Director of the Fuller Youth Institute and author of *Sticky Faith*

Preface

Originally, I wrote a book in March 2010 that was intended as a free resource for Frontline Community Church, where I've been on staff since 2008. A friend gave me the idea to write a "manifesto" where I could share the vision of where we were headed as a church and provide a common language for our community to use as we walked through the process of joining generations. We had two rules: It needed to be short and it needed to be free. Out of that conversation came a short, 50-page manifesto called "Why We're Unashamedly Intergenerational." We put it online as a free ebook and the rest is history!

What didn't surprise me was the immediate excitement from our church community. I knew they were hungry for the concepts. What did surprise me, however, was the intrigue from people all over the country. Instantly, the resource started getting shared and downloaded by churches, leaders, sunday school superintendents, grandparents, pastors, etc. I realized that connecting generations in the church - being intentionally intergenerational - is something that's applicable to every church. It's something all churches deal with. As I write this updated version, my best guess is that it's been downloaded about 8,000 times. How cool is that!?

So, you may be wondering why I'm writing about this topic again. After all, "if it ain't broke, don't fix it," right?

Great question. Let me explain... Two years after writing that book, I shifted positions at Frontline. At the time, I oversaw student ministries (6th-12th grade) and my title was "Now Generation Pastor." In May 2012, my role shifted to oversee the whole spiritual formation (or Intergenerational) department from "cradle to the grave" and my title is now "Intergenerational Pastor." What's unique about this transition is that I've seen these intergenerational shifts from a full-time "student pastor" perspective and now I see them from a senior leadership perspective. It's made me understand, even more, the importance of senior leadership being on board for these philosophical beliefs. (If you can't tell, I'm trying to covertly tell you to get this to your lead pastor and/or senior leadership of your church!) Thankfully, I jumped into a senior leadership team that's been embracing these thoughts for years - I just have the luxury of reinforcing ideologies that have already been there.

Over the past three years, the conversations I've had with you about this topic have been incredible.

The things I've heard, and the things I've experienced, need to be told. It's time for an update. The concept of joining generations has drastically changed my life. It's drastically changed the way my wife and I parent our son. It's drastically changed the way our church parents our son.

There are things I said in the first edition I wouldn't say three years later. There are things I've tried that have failed miserably and things that have succeeded far beyond my expectations. As a result, when I wrote this book I chose to delete some things I wrote in Why We're Unashamedly Intergenerational, but I also chose to keep a lot of that content, too.

The intergenerational relationships I've seen or heard about over the years are inspiring. And the world needs to know about them, too. So, that's why I'm writing on the topic again. If you're already familiar with the first edition, thanks for reading some of the same content again, and for taking the time to read this version. If you're brand new to these concepts, I'm excited for you to dream about how you can join generations in your family and church.

I'd love to hear your stories. Feel free to contact me at www.matthewdeprez.com or on Twitter (@matthewdeprez).

Matthew Deprez
September 2013

Part One:
Looking Backward

Part One: Looking Backward
What is Intergenerational Ministry?

....

At Frontline, we are unashamedly intergenerational. I love saying that. I can't get enough of it. If you could see my face right now, I'm smiling. Before we get into the details on why, it's important to clarify what we're talking about when we refer to being "Intergenerational."

We often write it like this:

8 > 18 > 80 and 80 > 18 > 8.

An 8 year old can teach an 18 year old and an 80 year old about following Jesus and an 80 year old can teach an 18 year old and an 8 year old about following Jesus. It's as simple as that!

Intergenerational Ministry has become a buzzword in churches over the past few years, so let me explain exactly what being intergenerational is and what being intergenerational isn't.

About 4 years ago I was introduced to the Fuller Youth Institute[1], a research division of Fuller Theological Seminary committed to leveraging research to local churches. They were the first place I saw the word intergenerational being used. It was like a light bulb went off in my head and I remember thinking, "This is exactly what I've believed for years, but I had no idea there was a name for it! Over the years, I have had the privilege of getting to know some of the Fuller Youth Institute staff, participate in a year-long cohort with them, and have come to deeply value the organization. That said, we have adapted the term to what we do at Frontline. Throughout the rest of this book you'll see this phrase used a lot. Just for clarification purposes, when these words are used, this is specifically what I'm referring to: Students teaching adults and adults teaching students. Or young people teaching older people and older people teaching younger people.

What Intergenerational Ministry ISN'T

Intergenerational ministry is not multigenera-

---

[1] www.fulleryouthinstitute.com

tional ministry. This is a critical distinction. One of the most common questions I get asked is why I don't use the phrase "multigenerational ministry." I explain the difference in a December 2011 blog post I wrote on Fuller's www.stickyfaith.org called "All Churches Are Multigenerational. Few Are Intergenerational."

> Intergenerational ministry is not multigenerational ministry.

Intergenerational ministry is like the shuffle button on iTunes. There's an "intersecting" of generations. They're not merely in the same room. They've walked across the room to talk to each other. They know about each other. They're deeply invested in each other's life. Intergenerational ministry is when a senior in high school prays for a senior citizen in a small group, or when a senior citizen calls a college freshman to let them know they're loved and missed. It's when each generation knows the other's name. Or when a crisis happens in a high school student's life, they know they can count on an adult to listen.

Multigenerational ministry is like the repeat button on iTunes. There's no intersecting of generations. They're all in the same room, but each generation is avoiding each other (intentionally or unintentionally). It's like an awkward middle school dance where guys are on one side of the room and girls are on the other side. Both genders are in the same room, but they're not talking to each other. They're walking around the room but not across the room. Multigenerational ministry happens when children and students are sitting in the same Sunday morning service as adults, but neither of the generations have talked to each other. Nobody knows more about the other generation than when they started the service. It's when they don't know about each other's passions and hobbies or their separate struggles, hurts, and pains.

I don't want to diminish the concept of being multigenerational. I was recently presenting on this concept at a conference, and a person commented by saying, "In some churches getting adults and students in the same room is a great 1st step." I totally agree! It's important that they're in the same room. All churches will, at some point, have various generations in the same room. It may be a potluck, sunday morning service, outreach event, funeral, wedding or even a student ministry program with adult small group leaders. It's not difficult to get different generations in the same room. The difficult task is to get generations speaking to each other. Deeply invested in the other generation's life. Accepting differences. Realizing similarities. Relying on each other and praying for each other.[2]

---

[1]http://stickyfaith.org/blog/all-churches-are-multigenerational, December 2011

It's important we understand the context of what we're talking about when we use the phrase intergenerational ministry. Is the intent to have all generations in the same room, or to have different generations to speak to each other and build intentional relationships?

How Do Kids Teach Adults About Jesus?

This book is not an attempt to get children and students to "go first." Let me say this as clearly as possible: Joining generations starts with adults, not children and students. Let me explain what I mean:

Based on my over-simplified definition of intergenerational ministry (8 > 18 > 80 and 80 > 18 > 8) some of you may be asking what I mean when I say students can teach adults. More specifically, how do children and students teach us what it means to follow Jesus?

Isn't it true that children help adults recover what we've lost when it comes to faith, innocence and boldness? Kids don't come up with logical excuses about why not to do something. Kids just do it. I recently heard about a middle school student who raised thousands of dollars for an international mission trip. That's amazing! Kids are bold. And it's something adults need to learn from. Often times, kids don't talk themselves into why something won't work, how to get "enough money" or how embarrassed they'll feel if they fail at something. I think this captures the essence of a simple and innocent faith. Adults learn from other adults because of logical conversations. Kids live moment by moment, learning as they try and fail. Adults have the capacity to learn from kids by recapturing our innocence and faith, not by expecting them to preach a 45-minute sermon about soteriology or never do something stupid as teenagers.

While younger people can, and do, teach older people how to follow Jesus, I believe we must be careful not to place unfair expectations on children and students. The reality is, kids are kids. Developmentally, emotionally, cognitively and spiritually, kids are kids. Simply put: We can't expect kids to be adults because...kids are kids. My concern is, intentional or not, adults heap an incredible amount of pressure onto students by expecting them to act like they're supposed to be adults.

In Dr. Chap Clark's book, Hurt[3], he does a great job speaking into this issue. After years of studying adolescents, Chap concluded, "Today, even very

---

[3] http://www.amazon.com/Hurt-Inside-Todays-Teenagers-Culture/dp/0801027322/ref=sr_1_1?ie=UTF8&qid=1371046000&sr=8-1&keywords=hurt+chap+clark

young children learn that they are only as valuable as their ability to contribute" (Pg. 47). Chap goes on to say, "Those who were noticed intuitively knew that they were noticed because of something they produced, displayed, or created (pg. 49).

As ministry leaders and parents, we have extremely high expectations of our kids, don't we? Churches aren't the only culprit, though. This carries through in all facets of kid's lives today - from excessive amounts of homework, to sporting events, to extra-curricular activities.

That said, as you read this book keep in mind that this may be the most stressed generation of kids the world has ever seen. May we not perpetuate unfair expectations on kids. Adults, may we be loving, kind, gracious and compassionate to them. Most of all, may we be patient with them and remember it's our job to "go first", not them.

Before we go further, I think it's important to break down some misconceptions about the way student ministries have been perceived over the years. It's important to be clear that this is more of a "universal" approach to the way student ministries have been viewed, not necessarily every church context.

1. Youth Pastors have a hard time being taken seriously.

This has been, in large part, a reflection of non-serious youth pastors. If you ask people to describe a "youth pastor," here are some of the words that might typically be used: Crazy, fun, energetic, ADD, irresponsible, hilarious, etc. For the most part, (once again, this is not universal), lover of Jesus or spiritually mature are not words that are associated with somebody in a student ministries position. As a result, youth groups are often times not taken seriously. If the leader of a group is only interested in having fun or playing games, then why would people take it seriously? I can see why this misconception is so prevalent.

When introducing myself a few years ago, I told a person I was a pastor, and they responded back by saying, "Well…you're just a youth pastor, right? One day you'll be a real pastor." Ouch! Yet, this is what society and our churches often think about youth pastors and student ministries.

2. Student Ministries have been looked at as a "babysitting" service.

Once again, not universal, but this is more often than not very true. At Frontline, there are parents who want the very best for their students spiritually. I am very glad for them, too! When I was the youth pastor, I used to get calls asking how things are going with their students, if they're connecting well, and what we talked about at our weekly student ministry program so they can follow up with their student. Inevitably, though, I got something similar to this during the phone call: "I'm really sorry to talk with you about all of this. I don't want to be a nag." I always followed those statements up by saying this: "I am actually very happy that you've contacted me about this. What makes me nervous are the parents who I've never talked to – the parents who aren't invested in their student's spiritual lives – who could care less what we do with their student(s). I love getting these calls. It shows me you care, and that you're not simply expecting us to babysit your child." Calls from concerned or inquisitive parents actually got me excited! We need less parents who just drop their students off for baby-sitting, and more parents who are actively involved in the spiritual well-being of their students.

> We need less parents who just drop their students off for baby-sitting, and more parents who are actively involved in the spiritual well-being of their students.

3. Adult and Students hate each other.

We set the tone for what other people believe or

don't believe. If adults tell students that all other adults in their church can't stand them, students are going to believe that. And the opposite is true, too. If students start telling other students to hate adults, they'll eventually start to hate them. As pastors, leaders, parents, grandparents, and students, we have to be responsible enough to set the right tone.

In a place where the tone has been set correctly, I've never heard about adults and students hating each other. It's always been full of embracing each other for who we are, no matter what age. In that regard, let's actually start talking highly of each other, instead of tearing each other down. Remember: We set the tone for what other people believe or don't believe.

4. Students are viewed as the "next" generation.

People who attend Frontline have heard this one a lot because it's a misconception that we've tried to squash to death over the past few years. When I joined Frontline's staff in 2008, the official title for my role was "Next Generation Pastor." After a few days on staff, I sat down with Frontline's lead pastor, Brian, and said: "I'm not sure I agree with my official title. I don't see students being a next generation. I see them as a NOW generation." Thankfully, my boss is smart and he said, "Okay

– Now Generation Pastor it is!" And the rest is history! I printed business cards that said "Now Generation Pastor" on them. I was listed on our website as the Now Generation Pastor. Whenever I was introduced up front on a Sunday morning at Frontline I was called the Now Generation Pastor. Needless to say, we take this very seriously. Our new youth pastor, gets the luxury of this title now.

Sure, it's probably a dumb semantics issue. But I see it being way more significant than that. I tell people frequently I don't believe in the next generation, because I don't think they exist. I think when we call students the next generation, we're intrinsically telling them that they're not really a part of today's generation. Deeply rooted in a student's mind becomes an isolation, of sorts. It's no surprise that students who have been isolated their entire school-life have a hard time getting connected into the larger body of the church when they turn 18 and leave for college. It starts to make sense why 18-25 year olds are leaving the church in historic numbers. People have actually started referring to this gap as the Black Hole, because they're simply gone. (You can read more about these statistics, and their response, from Fuller's College Transition Project.[4])

> When we call students the next generation, we're intrinsically telling them that they're not really a part of today's generation.

---
[4] http://stickyfaith.org/articles/what-makes-faith-stick-during-college.

Regarding church, here's what interesting about this point of view: Everybody is a part of the Now Generation. Whether we're eight, eighty, or anywhere in between, we're all a part of something bigger than ourselves. We all have value in the Kingdom of God. And it should never be relegated to age. At the same time there should never be a "next generation" in ministry, there should never be a "has-been" in ministry. Let's own it - many churches have a tendency to think senior citizens are has-beens. We think senior citizens don't like music besides hymns, the preachers aren't relevant anymore, they aren't willing to change, etc. I think we all have to agree that an eight year old brings as much value to the church as an eighty year old.

> Everybody is a part of the Now Generation.

There have been so many churches splitting and fighting because of this issue. People look at themselves as being a young person church, or an old person church. But what if we were both? What if age didn't matter? What if we could all do something significant for Jesus at any age along the spectrum? Brian, Frontline's lead pastor, said it brilliantly to me the other day. He said "Matthew, I don't want to be an old person church. I don't want to be a young person church. I want to be an intergenerational church." Amazing! So refreshing to hear. Basically what he's saying is that he sees an equality in the Kingdom of God that isn't based upon age, but upon the fact that people are simply human beings. We are all equal, and the instant that we relegate people being able to do ministry at a specific age is the instant we've missed out on the larger picture of the Kingdom of God. Age isn't an issue – And that's why everybody is a part of the Now Generation.

Students Need To Be Taken Seriously

With that said, can you see how students would all of a sudden be taken very seriously? If a student has value, and people believe they can be a part of changing the world while they're 8 years old, all of a sudden their input matters, doesn't it? No longer does a church want to isolate or separate their ministries. They see them as being intrinsically connected.

We refer to this as "silos" at Frontline. Farms use silos to hold different types of grain or seed. Each silo holds a different object.

Sir Ken Robinson (of "TED-talk" fame) talks about this split in our educational systems and how it manifests itself in our world today. Watch this talk to hear more of his thoughts about these shifts[5].

In educational systems around the world, we've adapted a similar model of organizing and splitting up children into easily managed "systems." For the most part, this has worked, hasn't it? During the Industrial Revolution, our educational system got flipped on top of its head when we removed the "one-classroom" approach to teach our children and broke them up by ages and grade-levels. This has been an important shift because we now know that children and students develop at different age-levels. My two-year old son is learning how to count to 10, while a middle-school student is learning algebra with those numbers, and a high school student is learning calculus with those same numbers.

I was recently at the Smithsonian's Natural History Museum in DC and saw this kind of "organizing" on full display. I remember walking into an exhibit that focused entirely on the sea. At first there were huge whales everywhere, then smaller whales (if there really is such a thing), then dolphins, then smaller fish, and smaller fish, then similar-colored fish, until eventually we were looking into microscopes at tiny particles of plankton and algae that live in the ocean.

---

[5] http://www.youtube.com/watch?v=zDZFcDGpL4U

The butterfly exhibit was the same way. It started with the largest butterflies pinned to the wall, then came all the blue butterflies, organized largest to smallest. Next were yellow butterflies…you get the picture. It's in the museum's best interest to organize this way, otherwise it would be totally chaotic to view. Each section or room has its own item, animal, or genus to display.

The problem is, immediately when we step outside the walls of the museum, our world isn't organized that way, is it? I'm pretty sure blue butterflies don't rule one section of the National Mall in DC like the Mafia. Blue butterflies are flying around yellow butterflies. Crows are flying around pigeons. It's all one big jumbled compilation of animals flying around together. And the ocean isn't separated by older fish and younger fish swimming in certain territories of the ocean. I'm pretty sure senior citizen fish don't claim the northern Atlantic while teenage fish only claim the southern Atlantic. (Unless Finding Nemo is right, in which case it totally destroys my point).

Now, obviously fluttering butterflies and swimming fish are different than a child's educational development, but it makes sense as to why the Smithsonian might separate and organize things the way they do.

We have done a similar thing with ministries in the church. Some of it has been good, and some of it is disconcerting. My question is simple: Have we erred more on the side of separation, but we need to integrate more?

Churches have separate ministry silos: children's ministry, student ministry, young adults ministry, adult small groups, senior citizens ministry (which was called Apple of Gold in the 1st church I worked at), and a plethora of other age-specific things. None of these age-appropriate ministries are intrinsically bad, as we'll talk about this more in Part III of the book. In fact, in some ways, these separate ministries are very helpful to our churches and congregation's spiritual development. That said, we must be cautious of existing in a way that we never integrate different ministries. Simple things like transitioning a child into student ministry as they get older go much smoother when the two departments are working together.

While we have separate ministries like children, students, young adults, small groups, etc., Frontline sees them being directly connected on a larger level. Why can't a student be connected into an adult small group? Why can't a child share a story of life change during our Sunday morning service with adults? Why can't an adult serve in student ministries? All age-groups can, on some level, be connected into all ministries. At Frontline, if we see ourselves becoming unhealthy silos, we have permission to call each other out. It keeps a healthy perspective that we're all connected into something larger at Frontline.

> While we have separate ministries like children, students, young adults, small groups, etc., Frontline sees them being directly connected on a larger level.

When we're connected to a larger picture, we all have a voice. This is why churches that are serious about the integration of all age groups don't struggle with the Black Hole as much. According to research from Fuller and Lifeway (www.lifeway.com), students who feel connected at an early age to the larger body of the church will often times stay in church when they graduate from high school. Compare that to students who don't feel connected to the larger body of the church, and you see faith retention numbers drop. It's no wonder why my small, country church has sent so many people into full-time ministry. In smaller churches, all people often have is the larger body to connect. In bigger churches (much like Frontline), each individual ministry becomes professionalized and separated. This is why we're so careful not to isolate and silo ourselves. It's too easy to do. And thankfully, we have a group of people in leadership serious about making sure this doesn't happen.

So...that's the back story. Let's get into some crucial reasons why I'm obsessed with joining generations. It's time to see how the Bible takes all ages seriously.

Reflections questions as you "Look Back"

1. What are some misconceptions you've seen as it relates to joining generations?

2. In what ways have you experienced multigenerational ministry?

3. In what ways have you experienced intergenerational ministry?

4. How have younger people helped you recover the innocence of your faith?

5. How do you balance the tension of placing high expectations on children while also expecting them to take their faith seriously?

6. In what ways are separate ministry silos good in our churches? In what ways are separate ministry silos dangerous in our churches?

Part Two: Looking Upward

Part Two: Looking Upward

God is Unashamedly Intergenerational

....

The Obvious Verses

I don't just believe these things for the sake of believing them. It's not as if I think they're just cool ideas. I believe them because it's a Biblical model for the way children and students are viewed. If you look in the Bible, you see an intergenerational approach playing into everything that gets said or done. God is constantly using children who are often the youngest and smallest in their family to do something great for God.

Let me show you what I mean…

An 8 year old kid was actually appointed king of Israel at one point (2 Kings 22:1). And it seems to have worked, too. It mentions that he ruled Israel for 31 years. Not too bad for a child that would be in 3rd grade in America.

And David ruled as a young kid, too. When David fought Goliath, it mentions that he was the youngest in his family (1 Samuel 17:14). Most scholars believe David was probably between 12-16. Once again, not bad for a student that could have been in Middle School in America.

Gideon mentions he's the youngest in his family (Judges 6:15), and then there are the disciples.

Most scholars agree that Peter was the oldest of all 12 disciples, and he was probably only 17. It would be like a junior in high school leading one of the most massive movements in world history. A small group of followers of Jesus has turned into some 2 billion living people professing to believe in Jesus. Amazing.

Those are just a few examples of younger people leading in the Bible. The Bible is full of old people leading, too.

There's Moses who rules Israel until he was 120 years old and scholars agree John was 90+ years old when he wrote Revelation.

So, I don't think there's any question that God uses any age-group He can to fulfill something great in the world

An Underlying Current

While those select verses are great to see, I think there's something bigger going on Biblically, though. I think if you look past what's glaringly obvious, there's an underlying current of intergenerational ministry that God wants us to see. Let me explain what I mean...

I believe even in the less obvious areas, God is showing us how to be inclusive in who we are as Christ-followers. For example, let's look at James 1:27:

"Religion that God our Father accepts as pure and faultless is this: to look after orphans and widows in their distress..." (NIV)

At first glance, it seems as though James is simply talking about taking care of specific people groups, right? While this is true, I think there's something much bigger going on. Think about the people groups he mentions: Widows and Orphans. I would argue that widows and orphans are quite possibly the most needy people-groups in the world. Widows and orphans have lost so much. But here's what's even more fascinating: Think about who takes care of widows and orphans? For the most part, the only people able to take care of orphans are people older than them. And for widows, for the most part, the only people who are able to take care of them are younger people. So these aren't just two random people groups.

What if James is saying there needs to be an "inclusivity" in how we take care of each other? I wonder if James is basically saying, "Young people, take care of widows. Older people, take care of orphans." This includes everybody on the planet.

Could this be a picture of what the most healthy churches look like? The most healthy churches seems to be churches that span all age-groups – Where adults realize that children are valuable to take care of them, and children realize that adults are valuable to take care of them.

> The most healthy churches seems to be churches that span all age-groups

And this whole "widows and orphans" concept appears all over the Bible! (A couple more examples: Deuteronomy 10:18, 27:19; Exodus 22:22). It seems as though God is lumping together these people groups for a reason. And while I believe God is very serious about actually taking care of widows and orphans, I wonder if He's trying to teach us that we all need to take care of each other? Think back to what James says is "pure and faultless" religion. He says it's taking care of widows and orphans. Could it be that what James is actually getting at is the fact that when we love all people-groups and all age-groups we experience "pure and faultless" religion?

Relearning What We've Already Learned

This sort of thinking is completely along the lines of Jesus' life, too. I love the way Mark chooses to explain what's happening when the disciples rebuke people for bringing children to Jesus. Mark 10:13-16 says:

"People were bringing little children to Jesus to have him touch them, but the disciples rebuked them. When Jesus saw this, he was indignant. He said to them, 'Let the little children come to me, and do not hinder them, for the kingdom of God belongs to such as these. I tell you the truth, anyone who will not receive the kingdom of God like a little child will never enter it.' And he took the children in his arms, put his hands on them and blessed them." (NIV)

A couple things to note here:
1. Jesus gets "indignant"

This isn't just Jesus getting mad. He's "indignant." But it might not be what you initially think it means. For a better understanding of what's happening here, we need to see the original Greek. The Greek word used here is "aganakteo." Our initial inclination is to just assume that Jesus is furious with the disciples. While this is probably true, I think there's something much bigger going on.

The Greek word "aganakteo" actually comes from two roots in Greek. "Agan" means much and "Achthos" means grief. So the way this could be translated into English is this: "...But the disciples rebuked them. When Jesus saw this, He had 'much grief.'" It's quite a different picture than seeing Jesus in a fit of rage, isn't it? When children aren't included in the Kingdom of God, Jesus is actually deeply grieved.

> When children aren't included in the Kingdom of God, Jesus is actually deeply grieved.

2. The word "bless" is a loaded term.

I think when we read this, we're just assuming that Jesus went around "wishing the best for children." And while this is true, (obviously Jesus wanted what was best for children), once again, there's a deeper meaning here. Historically, laying hands on people was a sign of ordaining or commissioning people for a new responsibility. Some theologians seem to think that when Jesus was laying hands on children, His intent was actually commissioning them to be followers of Him. Maybe we could look at the blessing that Jesus is doing like this: Children, you are blessed to be a blessing to others.

And being blessed by children is an incredible thing, too.

I love when children experience new things. An onlooker can't help but get excited about a child's new experience, can they? I recently asked a friend what he loves about being a Dad, and he replied by saying, "I love watching my kids experience things that I experienced a long time ago. It's like I get to experience it all over again in a brand new way." Children are a blessing, aren't they? It's because we get to experience things all over again that we've taken for granted as we've gotten older.

In some ways, I wish I could relearn most of what I've already learned about being a follower of Jesus. For this reason, I love seeing children and students learning new things about Jesus every day. My fear is that if I'm away from children and students for too long, I may start taking every day things for granted. I fear becoming callous and not wanting to learn. Children are constantly learning and constantly experiencing. Jesus deeply understands the value of being around children. And He believes they can bless adults right now. Not later.

Children bless me way more than I bless them. As I mentioned before, this isn't intended to put pressure on children to act or perform a certain way. What I mean to say is that the whimsy of children is often times what blesses us.

I'm not sure where he picked this up, but my son has been praying every time he hears an ambulance. Whenever he hears the sirens, he prays in a way only a 2-year old can: "Dear Jesus, ambulance helps people's ouchies. Amen." Let's all say a collective "awww!" There's something so whimsical about that prayer. It's so genuine. He's not doing it to impress me and I'm not sure he even know what he's saying, but he wants people's "ouchies" to feel better. I've been hearing firetruck and ambulance sirens my entire adult life, but until he kept praying for "ouchies", I never stopped to consider praying for the individual in the emergency.

This is how we're blessed by children - through their whimsical, innocent faith. As followers of God, we should constantly be learning new things, experiencing new lessons, and being shaped into Christ followers every single day. Probably the easiest way to do this is to spend time with children…and become one ourselves.

Jesus Himself Learned From Older People

Dr. Kara Powell, of the Fuller Youth Institute, spoke of the intentional intergenerational focus in the Bible by uncovering something fascinating from Luke 2. Let's take a look at the passage first, then draw some insights:

"Every year Jesus' parents went to Jerusalem for the Festival of the Passover. When he was twelve years old, they went up to the festival, according to the custom. After the festival was over, while his parents were returning home, the boy Jesus stayed behind in Jerusalem, but they were unaware of it. Thinking he was in their company, they traveled on for a day. Then they began looking for him among their relatives and friends. When they did not find him, they went back to Jerusalem to look for him. After three days they found him in the temple courts, sitting among the teachers, listening to them and asking them questions. Everyone who heard him was amazed at his understanding and his answers. When his parents saw him, they were astonished." (Luke 2:41-48, NIV)

Some insights:
1. Jesus is in the Temple

After the Passover, Jesus' parents leave Jerusalem and don't realize Jesus stayed behind. It says they traveled for a day before realizing He wasn't with them. That's some serious parental neglect. Someone please call CPS! After returning to Jerusalem, it takes them 3 more days to find Him. If you're counting: 2 days of travel + 3 days of searching in Jerusalem = 5 days total. So, after 5 days, where do Mary and Joseph find Jesus? In the temple courts! He wasn't playing video games at a pizza party with a bunch of kids. Jesus is in the temple with the teachers of the law.

2. Jesus is asking older people questions

Luke makes a point to mention that Jesus is listening to the teachers of the law and asking them questions. Does it strike you that Jesus was asking older people questions about the law? As a 12-year old, Jesus is intentionally learning from people who are older than Him.

3. The teachers are learning from a "kid"

The teachers of the law were "amazed and his understanding and his answers." The teachers are learning from Jesus - a 12-year old. This one shouldn't surprise us. After all, Jesus is God-incarnate! What I love is that the teachers are putting themselves in a position to learn from somebody younger than them. I could be wrong, but my guess is that the teachers didn't realize they were talking to the Messiah. They probably assumed He was just a regular kid asking some brilliant questions.

This story is fascinating because there seems to be a dynamic in play at the temple where 12-year old children were engaging in religious conversations with older people. Jesus is learning from older people, and they're clearly learning from Him.

> Jesus is learning from older people, and they're clearly learning from Him.

Mosquitos in the Classroom

In 2006 I attended a conference in Charlotlle, NC, and was introduced to some of the next ideas by youth ministry veteran Kenda Creasy Dean.

Kenda talked about something called "presbycusis." Presbycusis is "age-related hearing loss, or the cumulative effect of aging on hearing." More often than not, it's found in men, and gradually takes charge of your hearing after the age of 60.

> Presbycusis is "age-related hearing loss, or the cumulative effect of aging on hearing."

Presbycusis is even more fascinating than you may think, though. Kenda went on to explain that Presbycusis is the most common sensory deprivation in the world. Everybody deals with it, but typically nobody knows they have it. When adults found out about this condition called presbycusis, they did something very fascinating. In England there were department stores that were full of loitering teenagers, and they didn't want them around anymore. A brilliant British scientist developed something called "Teen Buzz." It was a high pitched frequency only younger people could hear, but adults couldn't. When the "Teen Buzz" was played, kids would freak out, because the tone was so piercing. As a result, all of the department stores that had the "Teen Buzz" got rid of all the loitering teenagers, because the tone was so high. Even better, the adults who created it couldn't hear the tone they had created! (I'm dead serious about this! Google it!).

But, I am proud to say that teenagers found a way out of this. They decided to take this "Teen Buzz" sound, and turn it around on adults and teachers. What these brilliant teenagers decided to do was create a cell phone ring tone using the "Teen Buzz" sound, and they named it the "Mosquito Ring-Tone." These teenagers were able to use the ring tone in class, and the teacher wouldn't even be able to hear it. BRILLIANT!

Spiritual Presbycusis

I find it fascinating that teenagers are able to hear something adults can't hear. But doesn't the church often get "spiritual presbycusis?" The church has the great ability to not be able to hear God's voice after a while. Kenda posed the question: Just like the mosquito ring-tone, could it be that adults lose their hearing first?

> The church has the great ability to not be able to hear God's voice after a while.

I guess the thing I fear is that the older we get, the more we think we only need people our age to live life. There becomes a huge difference between living Christianity rather than just studying it. There becomes a huge difference between preaching transformation, rather than actually being transformed. It reminds me of the quote I heard years ago: "We're not going to win the masses to Christianity until we're able to live it." There is a huge difference between saying what Jesus said, rather than doing what Jesus did.

Let's make it practical to the church.

Shane Claiborne, in The Irresistible Revolution, says "I am no longer interested in the church being an organization. I am interested in the church being an organism."

The church needs to be something we are, not something we are forced to do. And I think until we realize that, we'll struggle as we try to "reach the world for Jesus." We need to figure out what it means ourselves before we go into the world to preach a message about something we either don't understand, or pretend not to understand. Soren Kierkegaard put it brilliantly like this:

"The matter is quite simple. The Bible is very easy to understand. But we Christians pretend to be unable to understand it because we know very well that the minute we understand, we are obligated to act accordingly. Take any words in the New Testament and forget everything except pledging yourself to act accordingly. My God, you will say, if I do that my whole life will be ruined. How would I ever get on in the world? Herein lies the real place of Christian scholarship. Christian scholarship is the Church's prodigious invention to defend itself against the Bible, to ensure we can continue to be good Christians without the Bible coming too close."

I think it's a massive case of spiritual presbycusis, and it scares the life out of me.

Biblical Presbycusis

And so I guess the question we need to answer is: If teens don't develop presbycusis until they're older, what do we need to glean from them? What are they hearing that we simply don't hear anymore? 1 Samuel 3 gives us a perfect illustration of what a case of spiritual presbycusis is all about. "The boy Samuel ministered before the Lord under Eli. In those days the word of the Lord was rare; there were not many visions." Ok, let's stop there. I always had the impression that God spoke to tons of people, through many prophecies all the time. To me, I guess I thought hearing the voice of the Lord in the Old Testament was common. It just so happens, however, that in my studies I found something very interesting and profound. During the entire period of the Judges, apart from the prophet in 1 Samuel 2:27-36, we are told of only two prophets, (Judges 4:4; 6:8), and of five revelations, (Judges 2:1-3; 6:11-26; 7:2-11; 10:11-14; and 13:3-21), where there was actually a word of the Lord. Theologians think there's a slight possibility that 2 Chronicles 15:3 refers to this time period as well, but it's doubtful. The word of the Lord really was a rare occurrence! In the entire book of Judges, a word from God only came five times! And so we have this boy named Samuel who is studying

> If teens don't develop presbycusis until they're older, what do we need to glean from them?

under a man named Eli. In 2:26, it actually says this about Samuel, "And the boy Samuel continued to grow in stature and in favor with the Lord and with people." If that sounds vaguely familiar, it's because Luke 2:52 says the same thing is said about Jesus. So there's this boy who we know has gained clout with people. Not just with people, though, but with the LORD. It seems clear that this boy has stepped out on the right path of life. If his parents owned a mini-van, they would have a bumper sticker that says, "My son is an honor roll student at (blank) middle temple." (I know, that was really cheesy).

Random Sleeping Place

Moving on in the story, something fascinating happens. "One night Eli, whose eyes were becoming so weak that he could barely see, was lying down in his usual place." Now, the Biblical writers are very clear when it comes to them wanting to get their point across. They do it in whatever way they can. Right here, the writer is clearly trying to get his point across. Look at what the writer says. Eli was "lying down in his usual place." The phrase "usual place" right there jumped out at me so quickly when I read it. "Usual place" has some significant connotations in the Old Testament. The same Hebrew word, "Maqowm" is used in Genesis 28:11 when it refers to Jacob sleeping on the side of the road. This is not a significant place. It's just a random place somewhere in the Temple. Not just that, it's his "usual" place. It's the place where he sleeps every night. And this usual place where Eli sleeps is some random place in the Temple. But moving on in the next verse it says this, "The lamp of God had not yet gone out, and Samuel was lying down in the house of the Lord where the ark of God was." While Eli was in his "usual place", Samuel was in a specific place. Samuel spent his nights right by the Ark of the Covenant. This doesn't sound like anything significant to us, but it was tremendously significant back then. The Israelites had a pretty limited understanding of who God was and where He resided. To the Israelites, they thought God only resided in one place, in one room at the Temple. They were convinced God's presence resided in the Ark of the Covenant, and guess who we see hanging out there every night? Samuel. A young boy who was ministering under somebody else. And that somebody else, Eli, was in a random place somewhere in the Temple. So the Lord calls Samuel. The Scripture says,

"Then the Lord called Samuel. Samuel answered, "Here I am." And he ran to Eli and said, "Here I am; you called me. But Eli said, "I did not call; go back and lie down." So he went and lay down. Again the Lord called, 'Samuel!' And Samuel got up and went to Eli and said, "Here I am; you called me." "My Son," Eli said, "I did not call; go back and lie down." Now Samuel did not yet know the Lord: The Word of the Lord had not yet been revealed to him. A third time the Lord called, "Samuel!" And Samuel got up and went to Eli and said, "Here I am; you called me." Then Eli realized that the Lord was calling the boy. So Eli told Samuel, "Go and lie down, and if he calls you, say, 'Speak Lord, for your servant is listening.' So Samuel went and lay down in his place. The Lord came and stood there, calling as at the other times, "Samuel! Samuel!" Then Samuel said, "Speak for your servant is listening."

So, something really interesting happens between God, Samuel, and Eli. Samuel is having these conversations with God, but thinks it's Eli the entire time. So he goes to talk to Eli, and Eli is telling Samuel he hasn't called him. I can only imagine what Eli's reaction is. At first he's probably totally out of it, and in his sleepiness he tells Samuel to go back to bed, and that it wasn't him. The second time I bet Eli was either frustrated or very confused. But the third time...I really think the third time is different. Obviously it doesn't say anything specific about what his reaction is like in the Scriptures, but when I read this story I sense an urgency from Eli. An urgency that says, Samuel,

GO! Don't miss this! Please hurry - this is serious. I would surmise that Eli was very confused as to why his student has heard from the Lord, and he didn't. I really don't think this is any different than our lives now, though. After all, Eli was in his "usual place". He didn't even give God the chance to talk to him. Samuel on the other hand, just a young boy, consistently put himself in the position to hear from the Lord. And how long had he waited? It said the word of the Lord was rare. Had he waited years to hear a message from God? It says in the passage that Samuel did not yet know the Lord. This is not a reference to him understanding who God was. This was only a reference to him not understanding God's voice. He had been taught who he was, (probably by Eli), but he wasn't able to understand God's voice when God spoke to him. He needed Eli's help in order for him to understand it was God speaking to him. This has tons of implications for us today.

Allen the Groomsman

The college I attended, Kingswood University, has a "Christian Counseling" major, and a man named Allen heads up the program. Those of you who know me well remember that I was previously engaged to a girl I'm not married to now

(Awkward!) It was a brutal situation that caused me to slip into a significant depression. After a lengthy pastoral internship I returned to school to finish my last semester.

I needed somebody to talk to, and I figured Allen knew what he was doing. I called to see if I could set up one meeting with him, and he graciously took time out of his schedule to do so. We had a great meeting where I broke down and unloaded all my junk right before him. It was a cathartic experience. He prayed for me and I left. About two days later I received an email from him asking how I was doing. Shocked, I replied back to him and told him I was still hurting. That same day he called me and asked if we could meet again. A couple days later he sought me out again, and a couple days after that we met. Eventually we would regularly meet for counseling once a week, and would even spend time together out of counseling sessions. We even ended up taking a trip to North Carolina together to visit some friends of his.

Years later, we still talk frequently on the phone and email regularly. Even though we live 1,200 miles apart, we are in constant communication. Here's the interesting thing, though: Allen is 20 years older than me. When I was listening to Nirvana as a little kid, he was probably listening to The Carpenters. (That's probably an exaggeration, but you get the point).

We don't share the same interests and hobbies. What we do share, though, is a common desire to have deep relationships. We need each other, no matter how old we are. And it doesn't matter if MTV didn't exist when he grew up, we still deeply care for each other.

> We need each other, no matter how old we are.

As it turned out, Allen was a groomsmen in my wedding as I exchanged vows with my wife. My wedding party had two 25 year old men...and Allen. And it was awesome. If it hadn't been for him, I'm not sure I would have ever been able to get married. The very person I have gone to counseling with due to a wrecked relationship was the very person who helped shape me into the husband I am today.

I need Allen in my life to grow spiritually. And the thing is, Samuel had to have Eli there to tell him it was the Lord. We need each other. We need each other to survive. We need each other to learn. If it hadn't been for Eli, Samuel may have never known it was God trying to speak to him. Thankfully, I've had the opportunity to see friends, family and a church that fights for each other. Recently I've had an overwhelming amount of adults tell me they want to pay a student's way to Never the Same Camp, an annual Summer camp in Indiana our students attend. Beautiful. THAT'S the kind of stuff we need.

We need adults fighting for the spiritual well-being of students every single day. And students need to know they're genuinely being loved and cared for. We need students to know that adults are praying for them on a regular basis. (Or dare I say, we need adults knowing that students are praying for them on a regular basis?) We simply need each other in everything that we do. "Church" can no longer about the isolation of student ministries versus "adult church" ministries. To be the church God really intended in the world, there has to be an interconnectedness and an inclusiveness.

And this is why, theologically, I'm obsessed with joining generations.

Reflections questions as you "Look Up"

1. What are some other Biblical examples where God talks about joining generations?

2. What goes through your mind when you process that Jesus learned from older people?

3. Like the temple in Jesus' day, how is your church set up for different generations to spend time with each other?

4. How do churches today reflect the Bible's understanding of joining generations?

5. Younger people: who is your Eli?

6. Older people: who is your Samuel?

Part Three:
Looking Forward

Part Three: Looking Forward
Practical Ideas and Thoughts to Join Generations

....

Now that we've talked about the theological implications of what it means to be intergenerational, let's dig deeper into some of the practical, conceptual, and applicational ways that we can be intergenerational.

Kelencia (Kel-en-see-uh)

In October 2009 some women from our church took a mission trip to Haiti. While they were down there, they met a little girl named Kelencia. She became very ill, so her Mom dropped her off at the orphanage where they were serving. At the time, she was two years old and wore size one diapers. Due to malnutrition, her growth was completely stunted. Doctors ran some tests and found a hole in her heart. They said that if she didn't get a surgery very soon, she would die within a year.

One of the women from the trip came to me a couple weeks later explaining the entire story, asking if students could help. I'll be honest - I didn't think there was much we could do. I knew the surgery would be very expensive, and my thoughts were confirmed when we heard that the surgery was $100,000.00. Adding to the fact that only six doctors in the U.S. did this specific surgery, the situation looked quite grim.

Somebody we knew called the doctors, and one of the doctors agreed to do the surgery completely free!

The only problem was that Kelencia was in Haiti. Our main goal then became getting Kelencia to Grand Rapids for her to have the surgery. This is where our students come in. We challenged the students of our church to raise enough money to get Kelencia to the U.S. She would need a plane ticket, passport, visa, temporary guardianship paperwork, and a multitude of other things. We launched this "idea" during a series of teachings in December 2009 called "Injustice. Over the course of three weeks, we asked each student small group to participate in raising money for Kelencia. Here's some of what happened:

1. Knitting Washcloths/Dish Towels: A group of high school girls had just learned how to knit,

so they teamed up with an adult who loves to knit at our church and spent two straight weekends knitting washcloths and dish towels endlessly. Throughout the two weeks, they went door-to-door explaining the situation and asking people if they would be willing to purchase their washcloths and dish towels. In the end, they raised over $200.00 by themselves.

2. Jelly Beans: Another small group and leader bought a bunch of jelly beans and created a "poem" based on the different colored jelly beans in the bag and how they related to Scripture. They packaged them in small baggies with the poem and story attached, and sold them to friends, family and complete strangers. They made $250.00.

3. Pop-Can Drive: In Michigan, we have the luxury of .10 cent pop-can redemption centers, which makes pop-can drives an easy fundraiser. Now, typically this wouldn't be a big deal, but… it was December in Grand Rapids. One Saturday a small group went door-to-door showing people the picture of Kelencia and asking if they would be willing to give cans. It was below zero outside! They collected cans for THREE HOURS! They went back out two more times. They raised over $300.00. At .10 per can, that means they collected 3,000 cans.

4. One non-Christian high school student named Joe has been attending our youth group for over a year. I was told by his leader that he went to a family reunion telling people that instead of a Christmas present, they could write checks directly to the "Kelencia Project." He gave away over $200.00.

5. A high school student named Chelsi personally handed me over $200.00 of her Christmas money, telling me that Kelencia needed the money more than she did.

6. A student named Ian was so profoundly changed that he actually went to Haiti in April 2010 with his Dad and a group of adults from our church and got to spend time at the orphanage with Kelencia.

We ended up raising all the money we needed (and more) for her to come to the U.S., get all her paperwork, clothe her (in the frigid Michigan winter) and feed her while she was here.

Three days after we had raised the money we needed, though, the earthquake hit Haiti. We didn't know for 24 hours if she had made it. Finally we got a phone call and were told that Kelencia's entire town was leveled, and she didn't make it. That night we made an announcement to the students who had just raised all this money for her. Words can't describe what that night was like. Students literally wept for hours. It was horrible.

Through all of that, though, I saw something in kids that I had never seen before. They wanted to do more.

They weren't forced or pressured to do anything. They wouldn't be looked down upon if they didn't follow-up. Instead, they asked what else needed to be done in Haiti. I genuinely saw a new kind of passion in students. A passion that didn't quit when turmoil presented itself. To be perfectly honest, a lot of these students had more faith than me. They asked what else needed to be done in Haiti. I genuinely saw a new kind of passion in students. A passion that didn't quit when turmoil presented itself. To be perfectly honest, a lot of these students had more faith than me.

Twenty-four hours after we made the announcement that she hadn't made it, we got another phone call from Haiti saying she was alive at the orphanage and barely had a scratch on her!

In July 2010, Kelencia came to Frontline where we had the opportunity (and privilege) to dedicate her, and have a student pray over her before her surgery. It was beautiful.

If you give students the opportunity to change the world, they will...

Redeeming FORT Bucks

Each week the children in our children's ministry, The FORT, can earn "FORT Bucks." At the end of our service, children redeem their FORT bucks at the FORT store, (which is basically a glorified "Chuck-E-Cheese's). Students can buy stickers, temporary tattoos, Chinese finger traps and a variety of other things.

A while ago, a generous volunteer started wondering how our children can give generously to the "least of these" in our world, so we sponsored a child named Bilinda at the same orphanage Kelencia lives. Each week this volunteer let our children know they could redeem their FORT bucks by giving directly to Bilinda. If a child chose to do this, their "monopoly money" turned into actual cash. The cash value of a FORT buck became .50 real cents that the volunteer agreed to pay out of his own pocket.

During a conversation with a Children's Ministry volunteer, I asked "what is the average amount of FORT bucks a child redeems?" Our volunteer said it was 3-4 FORT bucks, which means we're giving away a lot of temporary tattoos and Chinese finger traps. I asked a follow-up question: "Do children give to Bilinda regularly?" She replied, "Yeah, a few children each week, but it's not a tremendous amount of money." She paused a moment. "...but there was this one time...a 10 year-old girl named Maria came to the FORT store and told us she would like to redeem her FORT bucks. Excitedly, I asked her what she wanted to buy. Maria told me she wanted to redeem them for Bilinda. Even more excited, the volunteer asked how much she wanted to give. At that moment, Maria reached into her purse and counted, buck-by-buck, 128 FORT bucks." Maria looked at the volunteer and said, "I think Bilinda needs this money more than I do." What the volunteer proceeded to tell me was that Maria had been saving up her FORT bucks all year in order to give as much money as possible to Bilinda.

> *If you give children the opportunity to change the world, they will...*

If you give children the opportunity to change the world, they will...

A Tension: Together vs. Separate

Youth Ministry in the last 40-50 years has taken a massive shift in the way things function. Some would state that with the start of para-church ministries, (Christian organizations not necessarily connected to a local church), youth ministry started moving away from the connectedness of the "adult" church and more to isolated student ministries. This is not to say that the organizations themselves are bad. In fact, much of what they do is needed and very valuable. But when a student grows up isolated from the larger church as a whole, they have a different vantage point of what "church" looks like. Often times those images involve pizza parties and games like "poop deck."

Some isolated students will barely see an adult while they're in school. And if they do, they don't see what adults do in "big church". Because of these programs, (once again, not necessarily bad programs), it was great for a student while they were in high school. But the instant that the student left high school for college, they had no idea how to get connected to "adult church". Students don't understand why adults aren't playing "Steal The Bacon" or other youth group games at church. What has ended up happening is students leaving the church after graduation. Fuller's statistics, through the

College Transition Project[1], estimate that 40-50% of 18 year olds will leave the church within 18 months of leaving for college.

At my church, this is not acceptable. We are not "Okay" with this. The good news is, most of these para-church ministries (and a lot of churches) have realized this, but it feels like walking through mud. There's so much catching up to do, reevaluating programs, and teaching people a new way to think. Compare that with churches whose focus is being intergenerational, and statistics show that the probability of a student retaining faith after graduation is a lot of higher if they have intergenerational relationships.

According to a Lifeway research study, "Teens who had at least one adult from church make a significant investment in their lives were more likely to keep attending church. More of those who stayed in church - by a margin of 46% to 28% - said five or more adults at church had invested time with them personally and spiritually." The article goes on to say, "Anybody wondering if they can make a difference can stop wondering...One Sunday school teacher, one chaperone, one discussion leader, one person at church who clearly cares

---

[1] http://stickyfaith.org/articles/what-makes-faith-stick-during-college

can impact the course of a teen's spiritual journey."[2]

This all makes a lot of sense. When intergenerational relationships are at play, students are not just seeing their isolated youth ministry bubble anymore.

> When intergenerational relationships are at play, students are not just seeing their isolated youth ministry bubble anymore.

They see church as being something more than just playing games, eating pizza, and having a 5-minute lesson (that is often times poorly put together). For a growing church to survive, it is crucial for there to be a connectedness among people. As I mentioned before, there is a lot we can learn from small country churches in how to do this. In small churches, all students have is the larger congregation as a whole. In large churches, youth ministry becomes "professionalized", and often times the more professionalized the youth ministry is, the more isolated it becomes.

As Frontline becomes one of those mega-churches, this is something we can't let ourselves fall into. Rather than running through the mud and trying to catch up years down the road, we're taking an active stance that children and students can be a part of the larger congregation as a whole.

---

[2] Read the full article here: http://www.lifeway.com/Article/LifeWay-Research-finds-parents-churches-can-help-teens-stay-in-church)

Over the years that I have been hearing stories about intergenerational relationships, I have noticed something very interesting. In most church-related scenarios, ministry leaders are almost always watching mega-churches to see how they can implement their newest ideas. I'm guilty of this myself. But with these intergenerational shifts, I find myself looking more and more to smaller churches to see what they're processing and trying. It's not to say we can't learn something from mega-churches about this, but smaller churches seem to be able to join generations so naturally. I would argue that church leaders would see great value in attending a church service with 100 people to see how they join generations rather than attending a service with thousands of people and a lot of national exposure.

Cutting The Sunday Morning Programs

In September 2009, we made a massive change to our Sunday morning programming. We saw the destructive nature of isolated programs and decided that it needed to stop. We instituted intergenerational serving opportunities on Sunday morning for all students, and the results have been astounding. In six months we've basically tripled the amount of connected students by asking them to "serve" on a Sunday morning rather than sit in an isolated Sunday morning service for just students. Each week we're continuing to see those numbers rise. On the Frontline website we've explained what Sunday mornings are like by saying this:

Recent statistics from the Fuller Youth Institute (www.stickyfaith.org and www.fulleryouthinstitute.org) have shown that students who are in an isolated student ministry separate from the larger body of the church on a Sunday morning have a difficult time remaining in church when they leave for college. We see that as a serious problem here at Frontline.

There's good news, though. The same research shows that students involved in intergenerational worship and relationships tend to retain faith better after they graduate. Our goal is for your student(s) to be connected in such a way that students see themselves as a crucial part of what happens at Frontline. Now here's the good news: Statistics have also shown that students who are connected into the larger body of the church will more than likely stay in church when they graduate from high school. We call this "Intergenerational Ministry", and we're really serious about it. Students teaching adults as well as adults teaching students.

In that regard, we've asked ourselves the question: Can a student serve in the same capacity as an adult on a Sunday morning? We see the answer being a resounding yes! Since the fall of 2009 we've done the unthinkable – Allowed students to serve on a Sunday morning! (Shocking, I know…). And what we've seen has been nothing short of incredible. Students on Sunday mornings are serving in children's ministry, handing out bulletins, greeting people at the front door, making coffee, taking the offering, cleaning the floors, and the list could go on and on. In just a few short months, we've seen so making students take the step of being connected into a larger picture of a church rather than just "student ministries."

> Can a student serve in the same capacity as an adult on a Sunday morning? We see the answer being a resounding yes!

Since our Sunday morning services are conducive to a middle school and high schooler's spiritual growth, we ask students to serve one service, and attend one service. This way students are getting solid discipleship twice per week (Sunday morning and Wednesday night), and are able to put this discipleship into practice as well on Sunday mornings. Pretty cool, huh?

Is It Still Important to be Age-Appropriate?

I'm sure some of you are reading this and saying, "...but students learn differently than adults. There still has to be something age appropriate!" As I've talked through Intergenerational Ministry over the past few years, this is a something that gets brought up frequently. The answer is: yes, age appropriate ministry is still crucial. It would be ridiculous to think that a 3 year old would learn from a 45 minute sermon on a Sunday morning. In that regard, we still have age-appropriate ministries on a weekly basis. We run an incredible children's ministry that is growing fast. We even have different segments of the children's ministry that is divided by age. The nursery is in a completely different section than elementary aged children.

For students, this is no different. There has to be something for students to come to and still be students. This is where our student ministry programs, Ignite and Engage, come into play. At Frontline we run age-appropriate ministries for both middle school (Ignite) and high school students (Engage). We see them as basically "a church service geared toward students in middle school and high school." We take these nights very seriously, too. It's not something we feel like we have to do out of obligation, but it's something we do because we love It, and because there still has to be age-appropriate discipleship for students of that age group.

This is the main emphasis of discipleship for students. Students hear a lesson aimed at teaching them the ways of Jesus while they're still in school, and afterward students break up into age-appropriate small groups to go deeper into the lesson. What's been exciting over the years is that it seems like our age-appropriate ministry has grown because of intergenerational relationships. We have seen a direct correlation of growth with Sunday mornings to age appropriate programming through the week! This is exciting, because we see both as being an integral part of discipleship for students. As our website mentions, students get quality discipleship twice per week (one age-appropriate and one intergenerational) and are able to put their discipleship to the "test" by serving alongside adults on Sunday mornings.

To sum it up, we like to say it this way: "We need to provide age-appropriate ministries with intergenerational opportunities."

To The Senior Citizens

When I was in middle school, George and Norma Bates were on my paper route. At the time, George and Norma were in their 70's, living in a retirement community. One day I finished my paper route and returned home to a voicemail from Norma. In her sweet, elderly tone, Norma said she never received her morning's paper. Being the arrogant and cocky middle school student I was, I called back insisting I had delivered it. At the end of the phone call, I finally told her I would go to the store, buy her a newspaper and drop it off. I wish I could say my tone was nice, but it wasn't. I was ticked, and I let her know it. After going to the store, I went to the door, dropped the newspaper, rang the doorbell, and walked away. Norma came to the door and kindly said "thank you." I didn't even turn around to acknowledge her.

The next day, Norma was at her door waiting for me to drop off her newspaper. It was 5:30am. Thinking she just wanted to make sure her immature paperboy didn't forget her, I didn't stand around to talk. Again she said "thank you", and I walked away.

The next morning came and there she was at 5:30am, waiting for me.

...and the next day.

...and the next day.

...and the next day.

Every day, for years, Norma would greet me at the door at 5:30am and say hello. Slowly, our conversations grew longer. Eventually, I met her husband, George. He was a kind elderly man who walked and talked very slowly, but his stories were so captivating I listened intently. One day in particular, I remember she invited me in her house to give me a snack before finishing my route. We talked about her family pictures on the wall and I stayed for a long time before heading out (Did you catch the fact that it wasn't me, a young kid, initiating this relationship? I didn't want anything to do with Norma at first. The fact that she seemed like she legitimately cared is what captured my attention).

A few months later, I quit my paper route. The next time I saw George and Norma, I was 18 years old. The week before, I had just accepted Christ at a Summer camp and the next Sunday my friends brought me to Houlton Wesleyan Church. As I walked through the doors, the first person I made eye contact with was Norma. She came over and gave me the biggest hug you could possibly imagine. Norma started sobbing and told me she had heard about me becoming a Christian. She proceeded to tell me that the morning I forgot her newspaper, she committed to waking up everyday to say hello and pray that one day I would accept Christ. It took years, but finally her prayer had been answered. She didn't wait for me to reciprocate her care. She didn't wait for me to clean up my act. She didn't wait to me for to talk respectfully to her. She went first and loved me the way I was.

Afterward, I visited George and Norma frequently at their house and listened to their stories about following Christ during WWII, holiness, marriage, raising a family and a variety of other things. George and Norma taught me what it meant to always follow Christ, in easy times and hard times. They shared stories of successes and failures. They prayed for me to be a Godly man as I grew up. It didn't matter how often I heard the same stories, I listened intently to what they had to say.

I legitimately came to love George and Norma. A few years ago, George got very ill before passing away, but Norma is still holding strong. Every time I am home, my wife and I make it a priority to stop by Norma's house and bring our son with us. She tells us she cherishes those times and we reminisce about the days I forgot her paper and she started praying for me.

I am who I am today because of George and Norma Bates.

If you're a senior citizen reading this, who is it

you need to be praying for regularly? Are you waiting for a child or student to take the initia-

> Who is it you need to be praying for regularly?

tive first? Who can you influence? How can you shape their lives? For George and Norma, it was about persistence. They never gave up. A woman's prayer at 5:30am everyday changed my life forever.

-Matthew and Norma Bates

Legacy Will

Let's keep talking to senior citizens…Have you ever thought about your "will." No, not a will and testament like you may have already written. I'm talking about a legacy will. A friend of mine named

Alex Mandura works at College Church in Marion, IN. Alex is 34 years old and serves as the Pastor to Senior Adults and Congregational Care. Yes, you read that correctly. He's not the senior pastor. He's the senior adults pastor. A 34 year old oversees the senior citizens at his church. Take a moment to let that soak in...

When I first heard what he did, I thought it was a bit strange. But then I heard how intentional he is about connecting senior adults to students and it changed my perception. He and the church's youth pastor, Matthew Beck, work very closely together to forge intergenerational relationships in very interesting ways. Alex asks the senior adults at College Church to write a "legacy will." The point is to process how you're going to leave your lasting impact behind. This could be done by leaving your Bible or journal for a student to have after you pass away, or it could include what steps you will take while you're still alive to pour into young people's lives. It could include choosing some students who you will commit to praying for, mentoring, writing letters to, attending sporting events, and a variety of other things. Or it could be as simple as getting up every morning at 5:30am to pray for your paperboy who desperately needs your prayers.

> What should I include in my legacy will?

Here are a couple great questions I've pondered since knowing Alex: What should I include in my legacy will? Who will I include in my legacy will?

Students Attending Funerals?

One thing Alex and Matthew do that's fascinating is bringing their teenagers to funerals. When one of the senior adults passes away, Matthew brings willing students to the funeral to experience what it's like to process grief, watch how people mourn the death of a friend, or celebrate the life of a great man/woman of God. It gives students an up-close look at something they will have to deal with someday - funerals and death. It matures them in very interesting ways. They're able to hear stories about these men and women they might otherwise never hear, and it allows them to process what living an intentional life is all about. Students are able to interact with the senior adults at the funerals and show them support in a time where they need to be surrounded with love.

Out With the Senior Adults...

My church, Frontline, is a young, growing

church. On an average Sunday, we have hundreds of children birth-5th grade in our children's ministry. The average age of a Frontline attender is somewhere between 25 and 35. The demographic that tends to be missing in most churches seems to be very comfortable in ours. Meanwhile, the demographic that tends to be in most churches (senior adults) are one of the smallest demographics at Frontline. This saddens me. Thankfully, as we have made more intentional shifts toward intergenerational ministry, the number of senior adults getting plugged into our community is on the rise.

What I've noticed, however, is that we live in a world where senior adults are told they're not relevant anymore. As a result, senior citizens are thrown to the side in order to allow for a younger generation to step in. We're all guilty of this in some way or another, aren't we? My Mom and Dad, who both turned 60 this year, just bought an iPad. I struggled trying to teach them how to use it, eventually getting frustrated when they would call and ask how to do something. We do this when it comes to hiring positions, programming in our churches and a variety of other things. In some ways, I understand the shift to become younger, give new people an opportunity to lead, make changes, and move the world into unprecedented places.

But in a world where senior adults are being told they no longer matter and aren't welcome in our churches, I find myself rising up against society. I find myself fighting for senior adults to stay deeply involved. Whether we would admit this or not, our culture, and most churches, are trying to find a way to get senior adults out the doors of their building. We're trying to ask a different question: How do we get senior adults deeply involved in the life of our church? The reality is, we all want what we don't have.

In our context, I'm not worried how we will connect and engage younger people. I'm worried how will we connect and engage with older people.

In the same way people ask the question, "what will happen if we're missing an entire generation of young people in the church?", I'd like to ask a similar question: "what will happen if we're missing an entire generation of older people in the church?" We can't forget that we're all products of our past, aren't we? The value of wisdom and experiences we can learn from senior adults is crucial. As I read on a fortune cookie many years ago, "The philosophy of one century is the common sense of the next." We can't diminish what older people can do (and have done) in our church communities all around the world.

Your Child May Parent You One Day

About a year ago, I attended the funeral of a 91 year old man. From what people shared, he was an amazing man. A gentle man. A humble man. A family man. Since 2002, he suffered from Alzheimer's and his daughter, a wonderful woman from our church, became his full-time caretaker. Since 2007, he was confined to a wheelchair and required 24 hour a day care from his daughter and her husband. I was struck by something very interesting that day. At the end of his life, his daughter actually cared after him. The "parenting" roles reversed.

Often times there is a movement from being cared for to being the caretaker. This woman, the very person who he raised as a baby, became the very person who would look after him for the last few years of his life. It became very real to me that one day I may likely become the caretaker of my mother and father. And it also became very real to me that my 2 and 1/2 year old son could likely become my future caretaker.

What struck me was the relationship between this man and his daughter. This man loved his daughter. When she was younger, he would stop whatever task he was doing in order to be the kind of father that was always available to show love. He was always there for her. In the end, she stopped whatever task she was doing to show him love.

The relationship between my mother and father is no different. They have always been there for me. They have always loved me and they have always supported me. Thankfully, at this point in their lives, they are still very healthy. If I were presented with the opportunity to be their full-time caretaker, I would have no reservations to care for them. But I wonder if my motivation to care for them comes from my experience of being cared for by them?

It occurred to me that Isaiah will most likely take care of me in a way that is similar to how I choose to take care of him. I wonder if all of us would parent differently knowing that one day our children might parent us in the same way we parented them.

> *I wonder if all of us would parent differently knowing that one day our children might parent us in the same way we parented them?*

The Ship

In trying to advocate for all generations equally, I started asking the question, "What do we need to provide at Frontline that leads to the best possibility of faith retention?" From that question came the basis by which I oversee and evaluate the spiritual formation process at Frontline. The 4 elements of The Ship are simple:

Wheel - The wheel is what steers and guides the ship. It's not what moves the ship forward, but it's what keeps the ship on course. We want every person at Frontline to be in a small group with a leader that knows, loves, and models for Jesus for them, while that person is taking "next steps of future hope."

Sail - The sail is what moves the ship forward, and it's what allows the ship to pick up speed. We believe what moves the church forward is when all ages are advocated for equally by giving all ages in the church a voice.

Mast - The mast is what holds up the sail. As a result, the mast must be as strong, or stronger, than the sail itself. This is where we focus on parenting. We believe that the sail is held up by parents who are connected and equipped. Connected = To other parents and their child's small group leader. Equipped = To raise their child in a Godly, Biblical home. If a child or student attends and their biological parents don't attend Frontline, we process what this looks like from a "surrogate" (or mentoring) point of view.

Oars - The oars are the physical way we move about the journey of faith. It's what allows us to put our faith into action, and gives "legs" to the Gospel. Our desire is that every person who is able, serves in some capacity on a regular basis.

With these forces combined (yes, that was a Captain Planet reference), we believe we have the best chance for all ages to experience life-long faith.

Prayer Sticks

This doesn't need to be difficult stuff in order for it to be effective. For example, something my wife and I do with Isaiah that builds into the "mast" portion of The Ship came from Pinterest. (I feel the need to say my wife found this idea, not me!)

Every night when we put Isaiah to bed, we pray with him. We want to do our best to raise Isaiah in a Godly, Biblical way and praying together at night has become a time for our family to slow down for a moment. Isaiah doesn't quite grasp the concept of prayer yet, but he gives valiant attempts. One night he'll pray for "Grandpa" while the next night he prays for "Oink" and "Cow", the stuffed animals in his crib. You can clearly tell this is a meaningful time of prayer for him! Eventually, Isaiah got to the point where he would just look around his room praying for things he saw.

One night he prayed, individually, for the 4 walls and 2 doors in his room. Yes, I laughed. My wife, on the other hand, had a different reaction. She wondered how she could make our prayer time more focused. She bought a bunch of wooden craft sticks (the ones that look like tongue depressors or popsicle sticks) and cut out pictures of people who are meaningful in our lives. She glued the pictures to the sticks and just like that...prayer sticks! (Thank you, Pinterest!)

At night, we each grab two prayer sticks and take time to pray for the people on the stick. Sometimes it's Isaiah's grandparents and sometimes it's one of Isaiah's cousins. Sometimes it's a kid in his children's ministry classroom and other times it's a friend of ours who Isaiah sees on a regular basis. We have about 40 different people Isaiah can pray for and it's allowed all of us to be more intentional during our prayer time. It's also allowed Isaiah to know who we think are the most meaningful people in his life. He knows the people we celebrate life with and who we turn to when we're struggling. Like most children, Isaiah knows his immediate family, but Isaiah also knows a bigger set of people. We've called them our "family of families."

Adoption Letters

My wife and I had the privilege of adopting our son, Isaiah, when he was an infant. My wife was actually in the delivery room when he was born and the nurses handed him to my wife first. (I'll give you a moment to cry like I did).

My wife and I talk frequently about some of the ways we can create an environment where he experiences that all generations matter to God. On September 30th, when Isaiah was 8 1/2 months old, my wife and I had the joy of going to court as a judge legally changed his last name to "Deprez" and recognized us as Isaiah's legal parents. It was a beautiful day.

My wife and I decided that our first "act" as Isaiah's legal parents would be a church-wide celebration that culminated in a child dedication. During our adoption journey, Frontline and our families were a huge support to us. We knew over 150 people who personally prayed for us, gave us money, diapers, formula, and so much more. Every one of those people received a personal invite to this event.

But we gave them a homework assignment…

Everybody attending (children, students, and adults) were required to write Isaiah a letter in which they described what their prayer for Isaiah was as he grew up, and how they would personally help him learn what it means to be a follower of Jesus. During the dedication, some friends and family read their letters, and my wife and I both read our letters to Isaiah. The next day it took my wife and me over 3 hours to read through the 130+ letters that were written. Children shared how much they loved him. Students told him about the love of Jesus. Adults made commitments to always be willing to answer his questions. Simply put, the letters were amazing.

Isaiah will grow up knowing he's been adopted. We don't want that aspect of his life to ever be a surprise to him. But Isaiah will also grow up knowing about these letters and the people who wrote them. He'll grow up with an understanding that all generations have been significantly invested in his life from the time he was born. We don't want that aspect of his life to be a surprise, either. For us, one of the most important things we can expose Isaiah to is seeing that all generations have the capacity to teach, love and sacrifice. God's

> *All generations have the capacity to teach, love and sacrifice.*

Kingdom is intergenerational and our prayer is that Isaiah will see it in every facet of his life growing up.

Advocacy

If we are going to take these things seriously, and if we're going to genuinely work together in changing the world as disciples, we must start advocating for students. Steve Argue of Mars Hill Bible Church has used this language a lot, and he's absolutely right. We have to listen to them. We have to trust them. We have to take them seriously when they have ideas. We have to include them. Basically, we have to believe in them. The great thing is, if we're all a part of the "Now Generation," there's no reason why we shouldn't do these things already, right? The simple fact of the matter is that if we can all be Christians at any age, then we can all change the world at any age. Again, we must be careful to not perpetuate too much stress on students in a way that looks down on them if they don't choose to go first.

Typically, for most youth pastors, advocacy would only be centered around students. Historically, a youth pastor is only around a church to advocate for his/her students, and push their agenda on the adults of the church in order to get his/her way. Most youth pastors have a difficult time balancing the needs of both students and adults. While I was a youth pastor, I saw myself as being an advocate, or a bridge, to help adults as well as students. This has to be done in order to live effective intergenerational ministry. Nobody is better than another person, and no group is better than another group. That said, I was available as much for adults as I was for students. As the student ministries got larger, the need for more adults to be active on a weekly basis became greater and greater. In that regard, we needed to keep the communication open for parents and students to remain connected – which is why we advocate for students and adults.

Individual Students Are More Important Than Programs

Ian is another "Now Generation" pastor at a huge church that is obsessed with seeing students seek Jesus with their entire lives. A few years ago we were talking about why students aren't taken seriously and he brought up something I can't stop thinking about. He wonders if it has to do with the fact that often times student ministries are seen as a "program" rather than individual students. The more he talked about it, the more it started making sense to me.

What's fascinating is that, for the most part, churches don't look at spiritual maturity for adults as a corporate thing, do they? Spiritual maturity has more to do with individual lives as opposed to programs. So why is this not the case with student ministries? I'm not sure, but I do know that if adults were to hear individual stories about how lives have been changed it would make an enormous difference. What we need to make sure we're doing is focusing on the bigger question of how an individual student's life is being changed, as opposed to how a program is succeeding. And once we see that there's an individual behind the program, we start seeing things from an entirely new perspective. So, what stories of students changed lives do you know about? How can your church hear this story, or stories? How are you approaching ministry from a people perspective, not a program perspective?

Remember: Programs seldom change people. People often change people.

> *Programs seldom change people. People often change people.*

Kids Creating Their Own Discipleship Plans

In the midst of replacing the Sunday morning programming for students at Frontline, I started processing with students how they could take ownership for their own spiritual growth. I think one of the reasons why spiritual growth for children and students is so difficult is because students haven't chosen to own their faith themselves (Steve Argue refers to kid's owning their faith as "self-authorship"). More often than not, their discipleship is simply them doing what we're telling them to do. Can you see how this might cause a student to feel like they're being pressured to act like adults? Rather than us telling them what to do, what would happen if they could process it themselves?

So, that's what we did when we launched "Growth Plans."

Growth Plans

In 2010, Frontline decided to try individual personal growth plans and student profiles for every student attending our program. Yes, every student. How long did it take, you might ask? A long time. But it was worth it!

Students, Christian and non-Christian, were

able to prioritize the ways they want to grow spiritually throughout the year. It gave students a sense of personal ownership and they were able to proactively take steps closer to Jesus while building a relationship with their adult leader as they kept them accountable throughout the year.

After a year, we took these self-owned discipleship plans one step further...

Student Stories of Future Hope

In 2011, Frontline was invited by Fuller to participate in the Sticky Faith Learning Cohort, a collection of churches processing some of the same shifts we've been processing.[3] It was a life-changing experience for our team. During one session, Dr. Scott Cormode talked about vision. He defined vision as "shared stories of future hope." One of the assignments we were required to do was write two "success stories" about students in our program over the course of the next two years.

We wrote one about a student named Kathryn, and another about Kyle. They were both written after real students who attended our student min-

---

[3] http://stickyfaith.org/sticky-faith-cohort

istry program on a regular basis. Over the next few months something happened in my heart that I wasn't expecting. I couldn't get the stories out of my head. The stories wrecked me. Every time I saw Kathryn or Kyle, I thought about the stories. Almost four months later, I called Kathryn and talked with her about her story. I read it to her and waited for her to tell me it was creepy. Her reaction was quite the opposite. Instead, she told me how inspired she was, and how much it encouraged her that people were thinking about her and took her seriously.

This is where we had the idea to take these "stories" one step further. That June we met as an adult leadership team, and each small group leader wrote one story about a student in their small group. It wrecked the small group leaders. Then we started wondering what would happen if students defined their own stories of life change? What if every student attending our program took time to write a story of future hope? And what would happen if they shared those stories of future hope with each other? It got us really excited!

> What would happen if students defined their own stories of life change?

That July, while our students were attending our annual Summer camp, we made it a reality. Students took time to write their own stories of future hope and shared them with their peers. We had students committing to go into full-time ministry, leading other friends to Christ, and bringing their unchurched families to our church. The students dreamed bigger than I ever imagined!

That year, each week one or two students shared their stories of future hope to everybody else in attendance! It was as if these students were writing their own discipleship program right in front of our very eyes - and it was beautiful. We even processed what would happen if every small group leader wrote a story about every student in their small group, and every student wrote a story of future hope about their leader! When I told Brian what we were doing, he immediately started thinking about how our entire church could participate in something like this! The opportunities are endless. What I realized is that students have the ability to dream in enormous ways about their relationship with Jesus, and it has challenged an entire church to dream about their own relationship with Jesus.

That's a story of future hope.

Why Is This Such A Big Deal?

Some of you may be asking that question right now. Why write an entire book about all of this? Why change all the programs around? Isn't this really difficult? Who cares? Those are legitimate questions. With that said, if you were to ask me where the future of youth ministry is headed, I can't think of another option other than becoming intergenerational. I don't think this is some sort of passing fad. I tell people all the time that I'm not interested in creating something new, but continuing something that is centuries old. It's not as if we're going to look at things from this point of view for a couple of years, then decide to change it all up again.

All in all, here's the big question: What is the most impact we can make as we structure our youth ministry? As I reflect upon that question, I think intergenerational ministry answers all of the biggest questions concerning students remaining in the church once they graduate from high school. And that's what it's all about anyway, right? What we all want to see are student's lives being completely changed by Jesus both in school and out of school. In the end, it all comes down to living an entire life for Jesus. We're not simply interested in how a student can be changed now… we're asking how they'll be changed later as well.

This is why joining generations is effective!

It allows students to believe there's a place for them within the larger scope of the church after high school. And because we all believe in each other, it's effective. We're not okay with students graduating from church when they graduate from high school. At Frontline, we won't rest until the Black Hole is eradicated.

> We're not okay with students graduating from church when they graduate from high school.

Let me finish by telling 3 stories that hopefully sum up the main concepts in this book...

Story #1: What We Do Now Drastically Affects The Future

In the summer of 2004, I was with a friend climbing a huge mountain in Maine. We were about half-way up the mountain and were exhausted, so we decided to take a break. As we sat there, a man who had been climbing the mountain stopped to take a break and eat with us.

He was from Eau Claire, WI. During our conversation he asked both of us what we did. At the time, I was still a student at Kingswood University, so I told him I went to a tiny college in New Brunswick, Canada, called Kingswood University. His face lit up, and he said, "HEY! I've heard of that place before!"

Now, before I go on any further, I was sure he hadn't heard of the place. My college had about 275 students so I was positive he was thinking of something else. After a while he was still pushing the fact that he'd heard of it and finally said – "No, really, I've met people from there." He then proceeded to tell us a story about how a group of kids from Kingswood were in Times Square in New York City in 2001, and one girl named Sarin helped him carry some of his things to a subway. She mentioned she went to Kingswood, talked to him about Jesus for an hour, and told him she was on a mission trip to the city for two weeks. Well, it just so happened that I knew a girl from Kingswood named Sarin and I knew she had been to New York City. But then he said this: "I still think back to when we were talking. She made a huge impact on my life. She said some things that I'm still thinking about today. And although I haven't become a Christian yet, I still wonder why a random girl like that would help a random guy in New York City." Over two years later, I am having a conversation with a man from Eau Claire, WI, on the side of a mountain in Maine about a

10 minute conversation he had in the New York City subway with somebody I knew from my tiny college. Amazing...

We have no idea how our actions today will affect people years down the road. If we ever get to the point where we think what we do doesn't matter anymore, we've given up on everything.

> We have no idea how our actions today will affect people years down the road.

We don't know what happens to people years and years down the road. All I know is that if we serve Jesus, we'll make impacts on people who will still be thinking about us in the years to come. What we do now drastically affects the future, doesn't it?

Story #2: Dead is Not Necessarily Dead

Death Valley is one of the most uninhabitable and inhospitable places in the world. Located in Southern California and the hottest place on earth, temperatures frequently rise above 100 degrees

Fahrenheit. The hottest temperature ever recorded there was 134 degrees Fahrenheit. Known for almost no rain, Death Valley gets, on average, less than 2" of rain per year.

But something entirely unexpected happened in the winter of 2004. Record rainfalls during the winter caused nearly 8" of rain to fall, allowing desert flowers to germinate, grow and flourish in unprecedented ways. As a result, the arid, dry and desolate landscape was completed covered in beautiful flowers.

People from all over the world flocked to Death Valley to see this bizarre occurrence. Scientists realized something interesting: Death Valley wasn't dead. It was dormant. It needed something to come along and wake it up. After a period of time, the flowers went away and Death Valley continued on with its record-breaking heat. It remains dormant until something else comes back to wake it up.

The connection to following Jesus isn't difficult to make. Each one of us has the capacity for life, but we remain dormant until something (or someone) comes to wake us up. We believe that "someone" to be Jesus, the Messiah. For all who call ourselves followers of Jesus, we know what it's like to be awakened, don't we? Jesus awakens us and we bloom, much like Death Valley in the Spring of 2005. But the difficult challenge is to understand what it means to continue blooming, and to continue growing with Jesus and each other. And that is what this book is all about. It's about being awakened by Jesus and living life with people all around us who refuse to allow us to go dormant again.

Story #3: Taking It Easy

A few years ago, I had the opportunity to drive a Porsche. Actually, it was a Porsche 911 Carrera Turbo S, if you want to be specific. I was in Atlanta attending a conference and stayed with a friend at his brother's house. One day we were heading to a restaurant, but couldn't fit in one vehicle. David, the owner of the Porsche, asked if I wanted to go with him in the Porsche. Before he could even finish the question, I blurted out "yes!" I remember squeezing in the passenger seat thinking to myself "Porsche's are not meant for pear-shared bodies!"

David backed down the driveway, looked at me and said, "ready?" At that moment, David hit the gas and within seconds we were going 87mph (that's 140km for my Canadian friends). It was a mindblowing experience. At the time, I had a 2000 Hyundai Accent that shook violently at 70mph. I had never experienced anything like it before.

After riding through the streets of Atlanta for about 10 minutes, David stopped in a parking lot and said to me, "So...you want to drive it?" I think I immediately grew chest hair. Terrified, I said yes and we switched seats.

As I was leaving the parking lot, David said, "You have free reign to drive this car as fast as you want."

I pulled out on the road and got the car up to about 45mph. We were hauling, baby! After getting the feel of the car, I turned to David and asked him if I could give the car some gas. He repeated the statement, "Matthew, you have free reign to drive this car as fast as you want." I hit the gas and we immediately got up to 55mph before I eased off the gas. A few minutes later, I asked him the same thing and he repeated the same line, "Free reign, Matthew. You have free reign to drive this as fast as you want." I hit the gas and we got up to about 60mph before easing off again. It was such an exciting moment.

Eventually, we got to the restaurant and my friend said, "So, how did you do?" Immediately,

I piped up saying, "I did great! It was amazing!" My friend turned to David and asked him the same question. "So, how did Matthew do?" I'll never forget David's response. He said, "Yeah, he did alright. He took it easy." Immediately my heart sank. "He took it easy?", I thought to myself. That statement didn't settle well with me. It bothered me the whole night and into the next day, until I realized why it bothered me. It bothered me because I didn't drive the Porsche like it was meant to be driven! A Porsche is meant to be driven like a... Porsche, not a Hyundai Accent. David had given me permission to drive his car, one of the fastest in the world, as fast as I wanted to...and I took it easy.

I don't know exactly what heaven will be like, but I have a concern. My concern is that when I get to heaven, Jesus is going to ask me how I did with his church, and I will excitedly answer, "I did great! It was an amazing ride!", but Jesus is going to look back at me and say, "Yeah, you did alright. You took it easy."

Jesus has given us free reign to drive this thing called "the church" as fast as it can possibly go. He has left us the keys, given us permission to change the world and my concern at the end of the day is that He is going to look at us and say we just took it easy.

For me, knowing about the research from Fuller, Barna, Lifeway, and the National Study of Youth and Religion, I can't help but think I've been exposed to incredibly helpful advice on how to help students experience long-term faith. And I feel as though an enormous component to providing long-term faith is through joining generations - intergenerational relationships.

> An enormous component to providing long-term faith is through joining generations

My hope is that we as a church decide not to "take it easy" when it comes to joining generations and growing together as a church. My hope is that we take seriously what it means to be intentionally intergenerational. My hope is that churches process what it means to break down ministry silos and barriers in order to see what it means to have age appropriate ministries with intergenerational opportunities. And my hope is that we see the value in learning about Jesus from all generations, no matter where we are on the age-spectrum.

And this is why I've become unashamedly intergenerational.

Let's join generations together!

Questions as you "Look Forward"

1. How have you seen your church join generations?

2. In what ways have you seen churches care more for programs than people?

3. In what ways have you seen churches care more for people than programs?

4. Who can you join generations with that is older than you?

5. Who can you join generations with that is younger than you?

6. What can you do differently to join generations in your sphere of influence? In your family? In your church?

7. How can you advocate for all generations?

8. What is your next step to join generations now that you've finished this book?

More resources on Joining Generations:

....

- Sticky Faith by Dr. Kara Powell, Brad Griffin and Dr. Chap Clark
- www.stickyfaith.org (There are parent and youth worker editions available).
- www.fulleryouthinstitute.com
- www.lifeway.com
- www.barna.com
- www.youthandreligion.com
- Souls in Transition by Dr. Christian Smith
- Leadership Journal – "iGens" - Summer 2009 edition
- Hurt 2.0 by Chap Clark
- Flickering Pixels by Shane Hipps
- Together by Jeff Baxter
- The Slow Fade by Reggie Joiner, Abbie Smith and Chuck Bomar
- Youth Ministry 3.0 by Mark Oestreicher
- A New Kind of Youth Ministry by Chris Folmsbee
- Four Views of Youth Ministry and The Church (especially View One – "The Inclusive Congregational View") by Malan Nel

About The Author:

Matthew Deprez speaks regularly at colleges, conferences and churches on issues surrounding family and intergenerational ministry. He is the author of four books and is currently on staff at Frontline Community Church in Grand Rapids, MI. He lives in Grand Rapids, MI, with his wife Megan and their son, Isaiah.

www.matthewdeprez.com
www.twitter.com/matthewdeprez

Speaking Opportunities

....

Interested in having Matthew come speak at your event? Matthew has spent the past 3 years speaking internationally to crowds as little 10 people to as many as 3,000+ people. Here's a sample of the kinds of events Matthew has spoken at over the years:

- *Weekend teachings/sermons at local churches.*
- *Seminars on intergenerational ministry. (Seminars can be tailor-fit to be as short as 45 minutes or as long as 6 hours, over multiple sessions).*
- *Summer camps or retreat with students.*
- *Trainings with your church staff.*
- *Trainings with parents of students and children.*

If you're interested in having Matthew speak at your event, visit www.matthewdeprez.com/speaking-engagements.html to see his availability and fill out a speaking request form.